W9-ALV-094

TAKE THIS STALLION

TAKE THIS STALLION

POEMS

ANAÏS DUPLAN

Take This Stallion
© 2016 Anaïs Duplan

ISBN-13: 978-1-936767-45-8

Cover design by Alban Fischer. Edited by Joe Pan. Interior by Joe Pan & Ben DuVall.

All rights reserved. No part of this publication may be reproduced by any means existing or to be developed in the future without written consent by the publisher.

Published in the United States of America by:
Brooklyn Arts Press
154 N 9th St #1
Brooklyn, NY 11249
www.BrooklynArtsPress.com
info@BrooklynArtsPress.com

Distributed to the trade by Small Press Distribution / SPD
www.spdbooks.org

Library of Congress Cataloging-in-Publication Data

Names: Duplan, Anaïs.
Title: Take this stallion / by Anaïs Duplan.
Description: First edition. | New York : Brooklyn Arts Press, 2016.
Identifiers: LCCN 2015028527 | ISBN 9781936767458 (pbk. : alk. paper)
Classification: LCC PS3604.U654 A6 2016 | DDC 811/.6--dc23
LC record available at http://lccn.loc.gov/2015028527

First Edition

To David

CONTENTS

TAKE THIS STALLION

$\triangle$ said to $\square$, "Did I hit an animal back there?"

$\square$ said, "No, don't look back."

ON A SCALE OF 1-10, HOW "LOVING" DO YOU FEEL?

I don't love Yeezus as much as I love
Yeezus when I'm with you. And rappers
get lonely too. Zip-lining is not
a cure-all. Kim knows that
and knows how to backwards-
straddle a bike like a real woman's woman.

I never got the message you sent me.
Where is the message you sent me.
Did you send me a message. Please.

      I bet Kim knows how to:

            climb trees
            shoplift
            speak Mandarin
            speak that language everyone's always talking about, the one
            they are going to put on the spaceship or already have

            For the aliens. So they know.

Can't believe it took so long for the waterproof phone.
Now no more excuses about I was at a party
I dropped it in the toilet
so drunk. Where is the message.

      I bet Kim:

            does Kegel exercises, knows Dr. Kegel, met him at
            a conference in LA

I bet Kim:

> knows who Molly is, knows the girl the drug's named after,
> knows her, knows the girl

I'm Andre 3000. I'm outtie 3000. I'm out of my element. I'm out of
cigarettes. I quit four months ago, it was never serious but every time
I tried to quit you'd call with something to say and that one time I tried
to quit and David died.

Benji at the funeral: This is so sci-fi.

> I bet Kim has:

> arm implants
> leg implants
> heart implants
> soul implants

> But they're all natural no chemicals.

A sage once told me: Your opposite is the Cock. Avoid Tigers. Seek a
Dragon or a Rat.

That sage got greasy real quick.

> I bet Kim:

> knows General Tso, slept with him, before Yeezy

Heard Drizzy mention Paris and it blew my mind. Did not know she
was still alive. All these years mourning.

I bet Kim:

> knows TMZ, had a drink with him, introduced him
> to Molly
>
> They're getting married next spring.

I wonder if Kim will introduce me to the love of my life. Where the
fuck is the message.

Yogi tea-tag: Love has no boundary.

> No. No, I'm afraid not.

Those poets think they are so cool because they know
the world is dying. They say Anthropocene,
Anthropocene. Anthropocene like it's candy.

> The Cock and I actually get along quite fine.

> > Atom, atma, atmosphere
> > collapsing
> > right over our heads.
> > The carbons
> > killing us softly.

I bet Kim:

> rips at least twenty mics
> on the daily
>
> That's a fair estimate.
> Not while Yeezy's home.

There is so much you don't know
about me. I once met an Australian,
told him he could have my underwear.
He didn't want it. I'm better
when I'm mysterious.
I'm better when I've had a few
days to forget
how much I want you
to want me like you want Kim.

Tell TMZ I said that. Tell him right now. Leave him a message.

How could your mailbox be full, it's made of stardust. #tbt: Once saw
kid goats playing. Remembered why I was alive. Have since forgotten.
Something about animals smiling. They can't do it but I swear to god
they're doing it.

How many days was Yeezus on the cross?

I bet Kim:

            stays cool under pressure, can deactivate
            a bomb faster than it takes Godzilla
            to kill the mantises

            Where was the sex scene.

I'm not opaque. I'm so relevant I'm disappearing.

Look for me with your hands
don't use the computer I hate
your screensaver when we're having sex.
Who has screensavers anymore.

I bet Kim:

> never kids herself, knows
> when Yeezy isn't coming home

Nicki: And get a dick pic and then you press send / And send a red heart and send a kissy face.

Our friend Bobby Frost: Something about free verse. Tennis with the net down.

I bet Kim:

> is a great doubles partner

Me and Bobby would've been inseparable. Probably not tho. Probably 75% match, 63% friend, 9% enemy. Take yr chances. *facebook guy*

Here's something I've always wondered about Siamese twins: everything.

Sometimes silence means
I love you sometimes
it means my phone is in the toilet.
How do I know which is which.

Show me the meaning of being lonely.
Is this the feeling.

Can't tell left from right
without singing that song,
the one about the loser.

We know so much more
about bullying now.

When we are all stardust, we will say *for matter*   →   the media distorts
the public's perception of ———————→   cosmic bodies.

Where is Oprah in twenty years. Will she have her own
planet? How did she meet all those doctors and why
don't the doctors on TV ever talk about
real diseases like gout and bladder
infections and I can't sleep on my back
because I'll drown in my sleep.

> You never shake me awake
> when I'm suffocating. Be a pal.

It's ok, it's not so bad. It is so bad, but it's ok.

Mirka in the margins: We can work with it.

I meditated so hard I lost track of my self.

WANTED: new self, must be beautiful
must be a real woman's woman (cf. Kimberly Kardashian)
must be implacable
must have heart as black as gangrene
must have sharp nails
must know the names of things

Re: those poets: So what Anthropocene.
What about the children, have you forgotten about the children.

My therapist is a beautiful man. I can say that.
It makes me post-shame.

John in the car: Something about gender and post-humanity.

I will always be a woman.
Even when I'm dead and made of stardust and then
even when I'm made of god dark god, I will still be
a woman just like Kim.

In two months, this poem is obsolete. VWLS R BSLT. "This poem."

All of Hannah's poems are about masturbation and she likes
my poems and that's how I know
I'm gonna be ok.

Bumper sticker: Musicians Duet Better   Question: Is it a sex joke.

License plate: KITTY   Same question.

License plate: CHOSEN

Yes, I am wheezy, but no, I'm not asthmatic.

I never lost respect for Martha. Getting arrested
is a rite of passage. That's why Canada
won't apologize for JB. Consider this:

> Baby, baby, baby. / Ooh, said JB.

> We lay nocturnal. / Speculate what we feel, said the other one.

> I feel good. / I knew that I would, said the first JB,
> the one before all the others.

Three things that make me a woman: Martha, *Cosmo*, Martha's pancake recipe.

Sex position of the day: Face each other. Do not break
                                  eye contact. Even as the water
                                  rises up over your heads. Even
                                  as the hypothermia. Even as the stardust.

Right now, do you like the drug's effect?
Right now, do you want more of the drug?
On a scale of 1-10, how "loving" do you feel?

Do you love me, do you
love me. Now that I can dance
with my eyes closed now that
I can ride on top no hands
now that my touch is so subtle
it makes you lose control now that
the blood the blood leaving our
bodies now that the corpses
are fully drained now that
the blue the blue feeling the one
with all the sharp edges / do you.

If I could meet with Martha, I would say this and first of all I would
not call her Martha to her porcelain face. I would say Miss Stewart,
how you've touched me. I owe my whole life to you, even these hands
these broken hands I owe to you. Would that I were in your shackles.

Insha'Allah.

We don't say that part but really it should go:

Hello, how are you, god willing.
Hi, I'm well, how are you, god willing.
I'm alright. Fred lost his job god willing

19

but we won't give up hope god willing.
I just pray he can stay god willing sober this time.

     I bet Kim:

          knows who Fred is, met him at Pacha
          did lines in the men's bathroom
          with Fred god willing.

I don't do hard drugs but occasionally
occasionally I do hard drugs but I don't
occasionally I like to put the fear of death in me
like to go a little too far
swallow a piece of glass, stand too close
to the microwave.

Balloons won't pop if exposed to direct sunlight but it's taken years
to learn that. All those years hiding my balloons in the shade.

Euphemism: Hiding my balloons in the shade.

     Something about orgasms or birthday parties.

Used to have recurring dream about demented carnival.
Ring around the rosie. Children with eyes too big.
The animals up and down in a circle, the skewered animals.
The parents standing beside their children on the skewered animals.

At the circus: The elephants, the aerialists. Imagine: a troupe
                    of aerialists called The Areolas. All different
                    kinds, some wide and pink. Some bumpy.
                    Some dark like rotting.

I don't do drugs but occasionally.

I promised myself I would never say "This poem" but now
look where we are, this sea, this sea of masturbation. Imagine:
a troupe of robotic porn stars. They form a union. In the future,
when the stardust, we will debate the rights of robotic sex workers,
will debate whether we are good people.

Sam at the gorge: I want to start an escort service when I grow up.

One way to tell if you are a good person: [blank field]

One way to tell if you are a bad person: Nothing makes you cry anymore
                                          not even the fact that nothing
                                          makes you cry.

Josh at the restaurant: Present shock.

Josh at the next restaurant: Present shock.

      I like when you repeat yourself, it makes me feel like a broken
      machine.

Would you like fries with your wine. Would you like
wine with your sex. How well do you think you could predict
the next earthquake, any earthquake. How much
do you think this movie cost to make. Factor in
the burning helicopters, the dead Juliette Binoche,
that quick reference to Mothra, did you catch it,
I say $75 million and on a scale of 1-10, I'm at
3 for "loving" and 9 for "hungry."

Feed me in bed. You know that's all I've ever wanted, Martha.

Are we still worried about apathy.

Mirka in the margins: POV?

When I smiled at that crowd of men,
I did not realize what it meant.

Remember when you drove by me and pretended
you'd never met me and then it happened again
at the stoplight and I got in the car and screamed at you
and got back out and remember?

John at the restaurant: You better order something or you'll embarrass me.

Mother on the couch: Don't fuck it up by being yourself.

Josh in the garden: Where should we plant the tansy?

Plant it here. In my eyes. I want to see flowers forever.
Flower highways. Flower Netflix. Flower plane tickets
to somewhere that's too far to remember
what you look like.

I'll never tell my therapist I love him.
That makes me post-post-shame.

Man in clothing shop: Lemme tell you watcha lookin' at. We got spring,
post-spring, summer.

Father in kitchen: What are you doing in my house?

Are we still worried about apathy.

John at the funeral: Everything vanishes.

> I was mad because he was so good. He was better
> than anyone else. I would've given him my heart
> if I'd known his was going to stop.
> What do I need it for.

Yogi tea-tag: Use your head to live with your heart.

> No. No, I'm afraid not.

The answer is GMOs. That's what *National Geographic* says.
The third world countries.

> Kim:

> > met GMO outside the apartment while Yeezy
> > was asleep, they smoked cigarettes, blew smoke
> > into each other's mouths

"Women's work": N/A.

I love it when they call a man hysterical, like they forgot,
forgot that's women's work.

On a scale of 1-10, I'm at
6 for "angry" and 10 for "bad person."

I've always liked the Christian Science Reading Rooms. Here are some
proposals:

> The Areolas Reading Room (picture books)
> The What to Do When You Love an Alcoholic Reading Room

Enough of that.

Here's to	harvest moons
Here's to	when you held my hand at Doris
Here's to	Jasper the cat
Here's to	white-on-white paintings
Here's to	government kitsch

I wish that Dan Beachy-Quick would write one of those drone poems about me. Something about how I never stop, can't stop, won't.

Not all my friends are dead. Only four.

Someone somewhere: It's not death I'm afraid of. It's the getting dead.

That's the fun part, tho, I think. You only die once.

Some ladies are scared to talk about birds and flowers,
but I'm not. Trust me, I know what that look means
but I'm more of a man than you'll ever be.

Augie in the studio: Don't get cocky.

I'm always cocky. I have an erection. It's for you / and you and you.

Mike in the front yard: She's a keeper.

Miss Minaj: Bitch, bitch, bitch, bitch, bitch, bitch, bitch.

Remember when you first learned it meant a female dog.
The exhilaration.

I've always liked Robert Motherwell. His last name.
Well mother, I suppose I'll be going now.
We've done all we could.

Kendrick Lamar: Pray my dick get big as the Eiffel Tower / so I can
fuck the world for seventy-two hours.

God willing. He meant to say god willing.

He has already been to rehab so many times.
Just keep him here, don't send him away anymore.

White people like to ask me about my hair.
They say did you get a haircut. I say no
it's the shrinkage. "White people."

Don't be so pessimistic.
Don't be so sensitive.
Don't go so slow do it faster
nevermind let me do it flip over.

I read an article about how violent
black people are. Black is not
an eye-color, no one has black eyes,
but it's an option you can choose
at the DMV, anyone can choose it. "Black people."

When I want to learn about being black, I look at the bottom
of ponds, where the trash collects and where the fish
with those sucking mouths live.

Just suck it be careful no teeth.

Eva on the couch: Vanilla just happens to be my favorite flavor.

Ithaca is the home of the ice-cream sundae.
Troy is the home of Uncle Sam. America

is the home of the brave
souls who go on beating themselves
over the back with talk of
the death of the dream.

When my therapist dies, no one else will be nearly as interested
in my dreams. I think about that.

Mother on the phone: Just cut him out. Just cut him off.

Enough of that.   Here's to   Martha Stewart, she's the reason
                                            John loved me. Something about
                                            a man his stomach, his heart.

The recession: Think: hairlines, the tide, our capacity for empathy.

POV? POV??

Plenty of Valium. To get us through. The interment.

Remember the cookies at the reception. Thank god willing
for white chocolate chip macadamia.

Why do you go on tours of cemeteries.
The dead people are not fun. Fun is key.
For example, blackout drunk, don't remember. It's like
sleeping but you're facedown in the corner
and the chicken finger vomit and I think
the nurse's name was Jenny.

Mike in the bedroom: There's nothing in this picture frame.

There's nothing in the frame
of this instant except
my hand touching your shoulder
but it won't stay.
Your body is so hard now.
They put on too much of the balm.
You've never looked so womanly
as you do dead now, dead the next day, etc.

When the stardust we will understand.

When the stardust the hypothermia will not hurt us.

When the stardust the blood the blood of the stars runs down your leg.

TAT TVAM ASI
"Thou art that"

I met god. He was my dog. We laughed about it.
Hello my loved one, I am drunk. I am
a circus freak. I hobbled up the road
just to see if you could see me. Blur me,
blur me, me. A tribunal of geese
told me to seek my father, to pen
a letter: Hello I am your spawn.
Wherefrom do I come. What's your nexus.
And the sky shot blanks shot blanks. I will die
here on this planet here on this blur, me.

AN ACCOUNT OF A CHILD BORN ALIVE WITHOUT A BRAIN AND THE OBSERVABLES IN IT UPON DISSECTION

I wept for the suffering of dolphins. By that
I mean the cicadas, by that the rained-over slices
of bread on the gravel, the birds that mistake

car antennae for homes. Do you recall
the words that god said. No.
How could you. It was all in tongues

and arms and legs. It was all
in those children's hearts, the screamers.
No more solutions. Only this:

my severed arms. Someone has severed me
for stealing the merchant's peaches.
Someone has hanged me

on a public street for slander. A common
mishearing. I said, There is no
hare on the moon, and they heard,

the tribunal heard. There is no end
to your hunger and fasting, and fastening
the rope, the reaper told me.

The mechanic told me to smile.
I did. He showed me his tongue.

THE INVALID

Daily, a man would come to my door to sell me peanuts. He had been punched in the face, time and time again. You could tell by the way he smiled. That was the most romantic part. His teeth like shattered diamonds. You have a mouth full of chance, I told him, and sucked on the peanuts' outer husks. You have a mouth full of loss. That was the most romantic part. It was the seventeenth floor, which is prime and unlucky. All things in their prime are unlucky. There were never any lovers in that hallway, not even at night, and you know you know what the night does. Peanuts never stayed the night. Just the please miss would you like to buy some nuts. Once I begged him not to go but he grabbed his gut like he had an animal in there. Once at a stoplight I saw him on the corner smiling his sweet mangled face at a lady with two children. I saw stars. The kind you see when someone wrings you out. I yelled to him leave me out to dry why don't you and you should've seen his eyes then. Since that day no peanuts but I adopted a cat and did not name it. That is my comeback, the nameless animal skulking around the apartment, the invalid. I make little replicas of the invalid out of soggy toilet paper and place them all around so the cat gets a startle here and there, seeing itself. Never saw Peanuts again but suspect he jumped off a bridge. My mother told me never to get angry at people because they could jump off bridges but she's dead so I'm back to not knowing anything. One day the invalid inspired me, how it ate at its nameless paws, and I burned my birth certificate. I come from the future. I told that to the man selling hot dogs but all he wanted to know was do you want any mustard. I wrote a song for Peanuts on the inside of the hot dog tin and sang it to the invalid. Peanuts, who touched you that way? That's as far as I got but someone told me it's all about soul and I still have one. The lady on Elliot St. tried to get me to see god but I told her I've already given everything I've got for a chance at the big leagues. She said when the rapture comes there will be no time for baseball but she's wrong.

THE WAR OF PARASITES

1. Song of Lieutenant *town of Babel?*

We warred without names.
Only the places where we fought
were utterable. The Isles of the Grey
Sea, the Stretch of Ossified
Wasps' Nests, there by the Half-
Eaten Strongwood. I became strong
as a fatherless thing, held my gun
to my cheek and shot at columns
of bone. My men were not
totally animal. Dog of theirs
that I was.

11. I Do Not Purport to Want to Stop Hunger

The captain had ordered a human tower
as such: thirty women, one holding
up the next with arms up-stretched. "You will scrape
the sky with your dirty fingernails.
You will dirty your fingernails
wanting the sky."

111. Eat Me

What is the diameter, ultimately,
of the puncture wound. Does the hand
there shrink or open, as a girl, say.

How much time between nail
and closing-up. I mean if you were to measure
the stigmata.

1. Song of Lieutenant, Flagging

The opposing faction called it the War of Dogs
not unjustly. More animal than not,
my men. We fought in places with names
impossible to recall. "George is lost. Bobby, Thomas,
and John have been shred." Dog of theirs that I was,
I became weak as a mangled woman. I slept
through shots. "I do not want bone, but rather,
a number. In how many fathers' beds have I slept?"

11. I Do Not Want to Stop. Hunger.

The tower's top is not as you imagine. I held no one. They were only
my hands scratching. "It could be," he said, "the greatest display
of love for one's country. To rip a whole in the sky."

□, AT RESTAURANT WITH ○

I wear gloves to dinner.
A mortician's blue
nitrile gloves. I wear
morticians' gloves
to dinner and I'm still smacking
of balm, having disemboweled
a septuagenarian just today
and combed his hair
and dealt him his shoes.
When the food comes, I still smell a little
like the viewing room. The peroxide
in the carpet detergent. The carpet
so beige, though all the time
people tottering
across it, all the time. Vertigo:
the tear ducts flood the inner ears.
And the cutlery is so charming,
I barely feel the heat
sinking from my fingers
into the fork, the fork sinking
into the fowl. It was probably
the size of the dead man's head
when they'd bent its neck.
Breakups are terrible.
Had it put up a fight?
The dead man did not
seem to mind the dress shirt

I'd picked out.
A tenable blue. It was
gorgeous, the white of his white
hand
against the blue.

BLACKNESS, WHICH WAS ALWAYS MOVING

In trembling over the damp
petal-mound, palm-cupped,
I could not but cry out,
stricken as the bird
who sees finally itself
reflected in the careful
accident of a bramble-knot.

THE FOYER FOREVER

Who is dead in the ambulance.
Is it you or me or one of our friends.
Answer me this: Who is dead in the foyer.
Who is dead on the sidewalk. Who, at the stoplight,
has left us. Who has jumped from the water
tower and left a note that said, Thanks

but I did not care for the weather. Thanks
but there is no need to call an ambulance.
Do you ever look for bodies on the water
or do you prefer to have fun with friends.
I saw a man blow a man at the stoplight.
Blow him to pieces. How many die in the foyer

at the hospital. In the foyer
of my apartment, I give my thanks
to the mold growing on the windows. Stop, light.
What time does it come, the ambulance.
I want to be sure to tell my friends
to come around once in a while to water

the hydrangeas. Or are they peonies, who cares. Water
whatever agrees to stay alive. Do not dwell in the foyer
unless to asphyxiate. No need, my friends,
for thanks and praise. We kill ourselves off selflessly. Thanks
be to god who does not dial for an ambulance
when the children are sick. I made a mistake at the stoplight.

I thought they were making love and could not stop. Light
punctures of intercourse. O genital fountain, spray thine water
upon my grave. Who is dead up against the fence. Ambulance,

you have taken far too long. I left a note in the foyer
that read, Thanks but I did not care for the food. Thanks
but there is no need to alert my friends—

they know. Remember, my friends,
it is near impossible to stop light
from entering you. Withhold your thanks
until the deed is done. Floating on the water,
you can sometimes spot a loved one. A foyer
full of guestbooks and black-gowned beasts. Ambulance,

do not come for me. Save my friends. Ambulance,
when will your engine stop? The light in the foyer, the light foyer—
In the night, I gave thanks to the water all around me, the water.

ON HOW TO WIN
WITH OR WITHOUT TRYING

Can't a negro get some chaos in here, David said. Looking for love, we stand by the church and mimic its stance. We explain to our friends that nothing is to be taken for granted, not even the fingernail clippings. We adjust our sex, our shapes, invent new sounds for pleasure. I say, My best deeds are slander, libel, and late night apology. He says, I'm not here for that. We don newer shapes. We study the voices of people diverging with scholarly disinterest. In evenings, I return to the church and lie at its base keeping in mind that the fingernails continue to grow. Clip them now clip them now, a wise man once said. I use an envelope to store the excess and keep this in my pocket. When I confess for the last time, I recite the pleasure sounds.

LA VUELTA

Hoping to start a riot,
the boy went on revealing his ankles
to the grazing stallions.
The animals bulged
in the sun and were blinded
by the sun. The boy's ankles were taut
and red. The animals grazed
in the sun and the boy
went on revealing his ankles
to the grazing stallions, hoping
to start a riot.

I once saw men riot when a woman
lifted her long black skirt.
He showed the way his ankle-bones
bulged and the men bulged
in the sun, and took to chasing
the boy, who went dashing, his skirt flapping, down
a lean alley, and evaporated.
When she was lost to them
they took to striking
each other over the head with empty fists,
striking until blood ran freely in the city
ditches. All of this sounding like horses thundering
into each other, peeling themselves
off of each other, and thundering
again. The whole city, this sound.

I AM AN ONLY CHILD
(AM I ONLY A CHILD)

Occasionally, there is a herd of mares outside my window.
They shout my name over & over. I say back, I say, I don't have
any stories to tell you. They become angry. They throw their
bodies at the walls of my home. Finally I dig a moat. I dig it
deep. All night, there are horses drowning outside my window.
They cry, How could you do this to us? They cry. I lower the blinds
& sleep for a long, long time. When I awake, my bedroom is full
of limp horse bodies. Who put these in here? Who?
But not a single mare stirs. I lift the blinds. The moat is empty
of horse bodies. The face of the water gleams in the sun. I leap out. I lower
my body into the moat. Finally I am alone, I say to myself. I dip
my muzzle & drink.

Dear △,

Looking down from the top of Victoria, I found ten thousand steel prisms. O Hong Kong! As I turned around, I saw the bodies of two Black Kites, which, overlooking the city, had turned to steel. I felt my body become cool and shiny. Do not look too long at the photo. You may find your limbs beginning to harden.

Yours,

□

PORTRAIT OF THE FOUND SELF

I hear only a bird remote
and laughing from beneath
its hunter's hands. The trill
is joyful. I become at night
the hunter whose hands delight
in the roundness of her animal.

I move to the window.
My gaze is soft. I see
my shadow from outside,
my shadow laughing
from beneath my hands.

HUNGER (MOTIVATIONAL STATE)

I become my mother and father. I don
their postures, I posture, "Where-
     have they gone and how do I stop them
from devouring me." The answer is
     unspoken but the gutter whispers
in the rain on the side of the house
     in which I live alone. I lock the door.
I sleep with my costumes on and my eyes open
     in case the wind comes rapping, wet
and full of gutter-sounds. In the middle of the night,
     looking for my childbody.

A FLEDGLING IS A YOUNG BIRD THAT HAS ITS FEATHERS AND IS LEARNING TO FLY

[1]

S-H-E-D-E-V-L.
I, on the other hand,
make sure to wash my mouth
whenever I say something slippery. I am washing
right now, ma chérie, with a pen
in my left hand and my page on the rim of the sink
and my right hand is reaching toward you,
you in the mirror, to pull your hair out.

[2]

The terror of having to realize the unrealizable: I am a baby
on the kitchen counter, one of many. My mother continues
to unload us from a crate. The counter is littered with knives.
No one is hurt except all of us are hurt and yearning
to sleep. It is cold. Keep this in mind, it is cold.
My mother, the woman, she is wearing a chain
of children's molars. A man wearing the same chain
appears in the doorway and begins to eat us one by one.

[3]

My mother in a blue apron. It is springtime inside
and outside the kitchen. I hear the dog screech from the yard,
his "body" is caught under the lawnmower
my father is driving. I tell my mother to get off
the machine, to let this one live, but he doesn't listen,
he takes off his apron and steps outside,
sees the dog screeching and by now, it is still springtime.

[4]

You are in control. The day is yellow
in the sense that the grasses are dying. There are animals
dying every minute, waiting, even after their deaths,
to be adopted. Pick up the phone. Pick up the baby
and set it in a meadow. Wait for a bird to settle
on its head and take a photo. Mail the photo to your mother.
Write to her, write, Just this once, just this once,
would you please come to my recital. I promise I will do better
than Jenny. Take the baby back into your hands
and promise me.

[5]

What makes us go all the way to the bottom. The brother had severed
one of his fingers attempting to slice a fig. The mother took him
to the emergency room but only the brother returned. Since then,
I have had to be the woman of the house. I am proud to say
that the brother's fingers have grown six inches since I took over and the father
is very well near portly. I promise to fill them up. I say this every time
I pass the emergency room on the way to bed.

[6]

At least we have our authenticity. This is the last time
I'll ever lend my skin to a man who tells me he'll give it
right back. Keep this in mind: it is cold and my eyes
are too bloated for my head. I have had to squeeze them dry
at day's end. I do this in the bathroom, where a lady is safe
to take her apron off and her eyes out.

[7]

I say to Michael, I say, Michael,
why don't you go out and find yourself a woman. I say,
Michael, any lady would be lucky to let you have her. I say, Take
this cake and take it into your arms and find a woman.

[8]

You are in control. Take this stallion and ride it
to your demise. (Read: the sunset, behind the stars,
the green green garden.) Compare my flesh to yours. Look at my hair:
my neck hair and my toe hair. (Read: I am a woman and a woman
is a woman.) My unconscious is under siege,
Papa Bear. Take up your arms
and throw them around me. Bring a bouquet,
bring your big cowboy hat. Show me how to kill a horse.

Dear O,

My heart is a stray cat, lounging beneath a bush at Myrtle Beach. You are the bush.

Longing for yr adoption,
◇

WHY WOULD YOU EVER GO TO A POOL PARTY ANYWAY

I.

Anaïs, you needn't cry
like a baby seal. You needn't wear
your hair long, just to divert
the passing sailors—
   O what flag waves outside the windows
of all fledgling girls
when they detect
what lives
between their legs.
      John Paul once said to me,
O Anaïs, o Anaïs, what lives between your legs,
and I opened up to him, put his hand inside me
and said, This is the fiery throat of God—be careful.
You may find you are no longer every-
thing you had been
before you arrived.

II.

He said, she said, we wrote of a great awakening.
Instead of death we only moaned
every time the sun did wane and how
it waned every morning. Today could be
the day that does not end
in your death-
ly embrace.

I FELT LIKE A TRAFFIC LIGHT AS SOON AS I GOT INSIDE YOU

I.

This is how to be honest:
I learned it on the subway: look
me in the eyes and tell me

I'm not beautiful. Sometimes
it's best just to drop out tune down
let go so ever so deep. So deep

was her throat and how the gods
did sing, how the dog doth sing,
Happy birthday, darling. And thank you, too.

II.

I met a girl named Martha
with eyes as big as Arizona,
relative to other states.

Martha, I promise to change
your bandages forever 'n' ever,
and if the doctors should ever say,

O Anaïs, Martha will not survive
without your limbs, I would
tear them off one-by-one.

III.

Lift me up—

I am looking at the neighbor's wife,
I am looking at the neighbor's wife
and wond'ring where she buys her things.

Lower me down, just below your eye-
level and tell me about the time

your mother made you wear clothes you didn't want to wear.

IV.

Never forget to greet the doctor in the room.
I know it was your birthday but I never got
the prescription you wrote me.

Dancing is not permitted in certain towns and that's ok
for some. Don't stop get it get it get it get it get it get it
before it gets you.

As soon as you walked into the room
all the flowers said O hell yes.

V.

My life is a ballad, it goes: O
ooooo! I can't breathe
when you hold me so

cold. Get paid get paid
tomorrow. Wake up get
paid tomorrow. You deserve
everything you get.

You don't know nothing and you never did, silly bill.
I don't have a gun but maybe one day I will.

A DEER IN ITS FIRST YEAR

A spotted fawn is dead
on the parkway. Discover
what killed it. Draw a map
of the wound. Discover the wound,
inherit it. A spotted fawn at the guardrail
of the parkway awaits. Discover
what caused it
to live: take the fawn
into your arms, dissect it
into halves: draw out the grasses,
separate the blades. Ask:
Is the ending ended now have we
surpassed it? Discover hunger, take it
into your arms. Wrap your arms
around yourself. Discover hunger.
A spotted fawn. If you are alone: give
your life to the fawn. Cloak yourself
in its undone ribs. Give.
If you are not alone: do not give
the fawn away. Leave it, take yourself.
Let your dress billow over
the carcass. The polka dots.

TRY NOT TO SMILE
(WHEN YOU'RE NOT GETTING
YOUR PICTURE TAKEN)

I am the animal who wants to hold you
in good light. Today being your big debut.
Today, for spectacle's sake, you lay waste
unto hunger. Until hunger, we had faced
none of the usual dangers. The wild blue

yonder could very well be inside the two
of us, you mumbled. You drew pictures of Kali. I drew
blood when I fell off my bike. Trust
being a luxury for the animal. I am

too dirty but only when you are too
high on coke to answer the phone. Whose cue
is this. Whose turn to describe the taste
of vogue. In matters of tangible time, I know no haste.
Conversely, in matters of sex, I know only that I grew
invisibly. As in, I am the animal's mouth in your mouth.

ALBUM: SONGS OF POORLY DRESSED BLUES

Baby, we're merging—
it comes from me
softly as we skirt
death, every last one
of its sixteen wheels.
If you break, I break.
God yr long skirt, god
yr wide thighs, & beautiful too
is the gull racing us. I turn
to see the crook
of yr neck & keep
turning, look out the back
window, see policemen
packed like factory chicks
into a black hole
of a vehicle. I'm trying
to disappear. You wouldn't
understand. It's a gift
for you. & god in her black skirt
will die too.

I THINK THAT I CAN LOVE IT

(Shuck)

Mary, full of rage
wearing a bonnet, carried
a bonnet full
of posies, a
bonnet full of ponies.

(Jive)

Pitch-black Mary told a lie,
told the kids to ride
the ponies, freely.
Blacky black Mary
told a lie, said,
You will be loved
by all. Even the nigger-
eaters will love you.
Black blackest Mary
wrapped a cotton blanket
'round her bountiful
neck, sang a song with her
dangling legs in the salon.

(Juke)

I saw the negress bathing.
I brushed the negress brightly
and when I did expire
in her, did see the borealis.

SONG OF □ AT STAKE
WITH FLOWERS

Clutching blossoms,
the dying man
burns with a last
glow. Arouse
my bright sorrow:
So that's a world!
I eat my fill
of heroes.

OPENING MY MOUTH, AND A REAL LOUDER CRASH

"The thing we think about must have subsisted during the act of thinking."
                                        – L.W.

A gun reverberates in my presence
and perhaps I say, "This is going to be

      Do the boogie-woogie, do
          the hootchy-kootchy!

like being alive." If we trace a tune we know by heart
the notes and letters pull poorly together and fade

      Do the wolf-walk, do
          the hustle-bug!

as though they were an ephemeral string
of rocks in a box. A skyscraper for the man

      Do the mackerel shuffle, do
          the stanky legg!

whose prowess won the battle of Austerlitz.
Someone fabricates, "The sleazy Mr. Felucca will come

Do the black-bottom, do
the shim-sham!

to squish me this afternoon. I am overripe." I ask,
fraying, "How long does it take to derail a train?"

MULE, THE ONLY MULE

A praying mantis has most likely seen god
        more times than you. As soon as all the boats
within the range of your eye have sunk,
        alert the girl in the lighthouse. She, in turn,
will burn the village down, just in case.
        I did not want for any of this to happen
so soon. I waited for animals to become
        other animals. Not without value are all things
post-mortem. Eat the flesh, eat it right.
        The woman's name is Margaret but we call her sweet
nigger baby. The woman's name is not
        important, not today. And we've never seen a night
quite like this, the way the wind cuts rivers
        across our brow. No one is here now and no one
will ever be here in time. It is not admirable
        to be abducted. I have never lied to you,
I have never lain with you, I have never
        said anything about war to you. O kid-killer,
lie here in the wild furrows of my vulva.

THE ROOM IS NOT COLD & IT IS NOT DARK

There is a girl in a red sequined dress
in the corner of my bedroom.
She has the most beautiful eyes I have ever feared.

I think I think I have never
had a dress with sequins like that.
She tilts her head & I am grateful. This is kind.

I know a tilted head
is a peace offering. It means, I don't want to kill you, I just
want to see you sideways. Or it means, I can't bear to look at you

right side up, god, the light when you're right side up, I can't.
I am still in bed. She is perfect. She doesn't ask me
to get up. Other girls might have asked

for food or a petting. No, she is quiet like a new bud, no,
she is quiet like a field of goldenrod at the end
of autumn & it's collapsing under its own weight. It couldn't

go on forever like that, the goldenrod, all gaudy & feathery
like that. No. She knows I am thinking about flowers. I can tell
because she is smiling. I know she loves me.

I am scared since love means losing your shoe & not knowing
where your shoe is for the longest time & never getting it back.
I ask if she knows what I mean, but I ask without saying it.

I mean I look at her & I know she knows what I mean.
She doesn't stop smiling but she looks at me right side up now
& I am scared. Her eyes are too much like rabbits' eyes.

No rabbit has ever looked at me but I know how it would feel.
It would feel like this. She holds out her hand, just the one, the left one,
& it is clenched but I know what's in it. I know she has a bird in there,

a little one. I know this because she wrinkles her nose.
The room is not cold & it is not dark.
The carpet is not soft & it is not dark. My bedsheets

do not fall onto the floor when I get up. Everything is ok,
I am glad she is here. Now we face each other & we are the same
height. She is five something & I am five something.

We have blonde hair & short arms.
She stands against my closet door
& I wonder if she put anything in there,

like a rabbit or like a gun. It's ok.
I want to get her something to eat from the kitchen
but she smiles so bright & I don't think I should leave.

It's rude to leave when someone's smiling. Her hand
is still there with the bird. I know it's for me, it's a gift,
but what's the best way to say I can't take your bird

because I'll lose it & where is my shoe.
Her skin is so white like the carpet & like our hair.
Please tilt your head. I don't say this but maybe I do

because she tilts her head again. She lets the bird drop
onto the floor & it isn't a bird, I was wrong.
It is a gun, a little gun. I don't want it. I say that.

Go to bed. I say that. You'll be tired in the morning.
Go to bed. She gets it, she gets
that I don't want her anymore but it's not because

I don't like her. I've never had a dress like that.
She's not mad. She leaves the way she came. Don't leave
the door open like that, close it.

◇ LEARNS TO PRAY, WITH ○

In the bell-tower, your eyes shone
more solemn&gold than the crucifix.
The house below began to smolder
in your glow, and my hollow muscle jostled
'round in my chest, like coins
in pant-pockets. The grey body of Lazarus
was not upturned so feverishly
as mine was, by your hands, then:
see the ruined wracks of my soul-shell
realign. See the parched rivers of my body
run.

I WEAR ALL DENIM
TO THE EGO CARNIVAL

I am an amalgam of approved parts. Is this beautiful.
Do my teeth shine when I bite my fingers. Last night,
I died to make my mother laugh. She passed in and out
of my room. Each time, "How do you swallow so much
sleep?" Each time, a little more belladonna.

THE FIGHT OR FLIGHT RESPONSE

I.

O my peach, choke me on the curbs
of Paris, over and over. Tell me you love me
love the way I look in my blue dress. Wait
and please don't slam the door when you leave
again. One last thing: Do you like my tight
sweater. Doesn't it fit me doesn't it fit me
that I am unsure of the meaning of balloons,
of party hats, of family. And what are friends
but deadweights, o god deadweights. I am glad
I could say over and over all night please baby.

I am lying at the bottom of this bush.

What I mean is,
life seems to go on
(forever)
when you're self-

a) loathing
b) duplicating
c) fulfilling

II.

Imagine we are trapped in a steel cage. It is in the middle of nowhere. We
are nowhere. It is you and me and a woman dressed up real nice. She looks
womanly, we both agree on that. The steel cage is not anywhere and the
woman, she's singing something about balloons or party hats and it's not
in English. We can't decipher it. She could be a bear. Are you listening at
all. We are in a cage with no one else but a bear and everyone else has died.
The cage, it is floating, but how could we tell without a point of reference. I
want to call you Jim. That's the funny part, Jim. We don't even know we're
trapped. We're asphyxiating and we don't even know.

III.

Repeat after me: I know what you're thinking,
you dirty bastard. No, I will not eat this ice
cream for you. No, I will not drive this truck
into a lake. No, I will not paint the world
in dirty rainbow colors. Everything is lost all
dirty all full of lead paint. I'm a jerk, Jim. Don't
tell your mother please don't.

THREE CHEERS FOR ALL THE BABIES BORN UNDER THE GEORGE WASHINGTON BRIDGE

I liked it. We had a good time. We got / fucked up. I liked it. I had a good / dream. I got fucked up / the dream-hole. What an endless / orifice. Will you tell me a story / tell it dirty like once upon a time / I fell down the stairs and hurt my collarbone. That's why / I point to it like Amélie and hope / you've seen the movie. You've seen / the movie where everyone dies / trying to climb to the top / of a waterfall. They didn't need / to climb it and I've never seen / the movie but I assume they all / just wanted answers. A toddler on the express / train put a note in my hand, it said / never to turn my back on a man / with a gun but I still haven't figured out / how else to stay alive, here. Here.

FOR MY UNDEAD FATHER

After I had dug a trough on the surface of the ocean,
my friends, the sea-birds, remarked that it resembled
nothing less than god's gullet.

I had not gone far
enough when I corralled the centaurs and charged
back toward Thessaly. That time, you did not see

or did not care, Father. This time, I am more brilliant,
even more brilliant than you
had hoped I'd be. What was your dream.

I filled the trough with imaginary gold
trinkets that I had stolen from imaginary gold
temples on my wanderings in-between

imaginary homes. I filled the trough with your body,
which I had not known before but had dreamed it
to have twenty limbs, all blue and swelling, and calves

the size of women. What was my dream.
I lay my own self in it too and my friends   the sea-birds
remarked that I had eyes like Jonah, before the whale.

Little did they know,
so little.
Did they know

for whom I had been digging. It is difficult to say your name,
Father, because I do not know it. No one had ever told me
how many limbs you truly had.

It was only when I saw you   for the first time
            at the bottom of the ocean
that I understood that you were nothing

less than god's child. Then I understood
why Thessaly had not moved you, and dug.
And performed the impossible and filled it with you.

Dear ☆,

I managed to dock the old thing at Aberdeen. I went wandering and—would you believe it—I found the Jumbo Kingdom and went to that restaurant, the floating one, remember? It's true, everything we hoped for is true. Plates the size of tables, tables the size of rooms, rooms the size of houses. And in one of those houses, I stumbled into a waitress holding two blue bowls, one in either hand. She dropped them both. I forgot to tell you, that day at the beach: your eyes like two bluebirds.

    Yours,
    O

THE FLYING PHALANGERS

You and I are filthy but it is
our filth. Look how quick the clouds
when you expect bad news. Here is
a telegram I have never received:
Please. Hold out hope. The best
is nowhere in sight. Why always enough
time for lonely but insufficient
time for full. My cup of tea held something
dead in it. The fly I named Henry
because it had that look. Remember
when the magpies muttered like toys
outside the cabin where we prayed
for no more rain, no more secret
wild animals. When you face the wolf
do not comment on the color of its eyes.
Do not waste time trying to find
beauty in all things. Reserve your awe
for mammals in flight.

ACKNOWLEDGEMENTS

Thank you to everyone I love and everyone who has ever helped me. Here is a smile especially for you. And thank you to the journals that have published some of these poems, sometimes in slightly different versions. In particular, thanks to *1110/9*, *Berfrois*, *Birdfeast*, *Dreginald*, *Ekphrasis*, *Horse Less Review*, *Hyperallergic*, *Jellyfish Magazine*, *The Journal*, *Moko Magazine*, *[PANK]*, *Phantom Limb*, *Souvenir*, *TENDE RLOIN*, and *Transom Journal*.

ABOUT THE AUTHOR

ANAÏS DUPLAN was born in Jacmel, Haiti. She is the director of a performance collective called The Spacesuits and of The Center for Afrofuturist Studies, an artist residency program in Iowa City. Her poems and essays have appeared in *Birdfeast*, *Hyperallergic*, *The Journal*, *[PANK]*, and other publications. She is an MFA candidate at the Iowa Writers' Workshop.

MORE LITERARY TITLES
FROM THE
BROOKLYN ARTS PRESS
CATALOGUE

All books are available at BrooklynArtsPress.com

———————————

Alejandro Ventura, *Puerto Rico*
Alex Green, *Emergency Anthems*
Anselm Berrigan & Jonathan Allen, *LOADING*
Bill Rasmovicz, *Idiopaths*
Broc Rossell, *Unpublished Poems*
Carol Guess, *Darling Endangered*
Chris O. Cook, *To Lose & to Pretend*
Christopher Hennessy, *Love-In-Idleness*
Daniel Borzutzky, *The Performance of Becoming Human*
Dominique Townsend, *The Weather & Our Tempers*
Erika Jo Brown, *I'm Your Huckleberry*
Jackie Clark, *Aphoria*
Jared Harel, *The Body Double*
Jay Besemer, *Telephone*
Joanna Penn Cooper, *The Itinerant Girl's Guide to Self-Hypnosis*
Joe Fletcher, *Already It Is Dusk*
Joe Pan, *Autobiomythography & Gallery*
John F. Buckley & Martin Ott, *Poets' Guide to America*
John F. Buckley & Martin Ott, *Yankee Broadcast Network*
Joseph P. Wood, *Broken Cage*
Julia Cohen, *Collateral Light*
Lauren Russell, *Dream-Clung, Gone*
Laurie Filipelli, *Elseplace*
Martin Rock, *Dear Mark*
Matt Runkle, *The Story of How All Animals Are Equal, & Other Tales*
Matt Shears, *10,000 Wallpapers*
Michelle Gil-Montero, *Attached Houses*
Noah Eli Gordon, *The Word Kingdom in the Word Kingdom*
Paige Taggart, *Or Replica*
Seth Landman, *Confidence*
Various, *Responsive Listening: Theater Training for Contemporary Spaces,* Eds. Camilla Eeg-Tverbakk & Karmenlara Ely
Wendy Xu, *Naturalism*

Brooklyn Arts Press

Brooklyn Arts Press (BAP) is an independent publishing house devoted to publishing books of poetry, novels, lyrical & short fiction, art & photography monographs, chapbooks, & nonfiction by emerging artists.

Visit us today at BrooklynArtsPress.com.